No Regrets

The Ultimate Guide to

MW01165626

More Buyers, More Bids, Higher Price, Better Fit

TABLE OF CONTENTS

Welcome to
Woodbridge International

By Ross Joel, Former CEO of BroadcastMed

WOODBRIDGE
International
Mergers & Acquisitions Since 1993

Ross Joel

The team at Woodbridge International asked me to write an introduction to this book and share my personal experience with you all. I cofounded a healthcare media company in 1993 and in 2020 worked with Woodbridge to sell my business to a private equity firm. That outcome is not extraordinarily unique when you consider Woodbridge has been helping companies like mine transact for more than 30 years. Where my experience may be a little bit different is that in my career I have experienced "the good, the bad, and the ugly" when it comes to trying to sell a business.

The first time I tried to do a deal was about 18 years ago. We worked with a small "boutique" investment bank. The firm worked hard and put together a solid "book" on our business, but ultimately it only targeted a limited list of strategic buyers. The result was just two bids and buyer interest evaporated quickly during some early-stage diligence. Unfortunately, our bankers did not have any alternative buyers so we suspended our sales effort. To our credit, we looked in the mirror and realized we had a lot of improvements to make on our business, which we did over the next several years. We then decided to try again. This time we hired a small investmenat bank with industry specialization in healthcare media. They targeted their dozens of industry contacts but only yielded one bid which we did accept. Buyer diligence was supposed to take three months, but it ended up stretching out for five months. On the morning we were to sign transaction papers, I got a call from the buyer and learned that its investment committee had

2

decided to walk away from the deal. I was incredibly disappointed, having spent months and months of time, as well as emotional capital and money, trying to get the deal done.

We had no choice but to get back to work. We made more improvements to the company and in January 2020, three months before anyone knew there was a looming pandemic approaching, my business partner and I confronted the realization that our career runways were getting shorter and shorter. We knew we had to come up with a definitive exit plan. We talked about selling the business to our loyal employees through an Employee Stock Ownership Plan (ESOP). Ultimately, we decided to go back to market one more time. We conducted interviews with a number of M&A experts, among them Woodbridge International. What struck me most about Woodbridge was their step-by-step process and their adherence to timeline in getting deals done. In my two failed attempts to sell, I had experienced first-hand that "Time Kills Deals"! They also approached selling my business like I had approached selling to clients—they considered sales a numbers game. They took our business out to thousands of prospective buyers. Ultimately, we received 34 bids. Once into diligence, Woodbridge held the buyer accountable and we closed in record-setting time. The terms of the deal were outstanding and exceeded my expectations.

I stayed on as CEO for 20 months during which the company grew by 10 times, partly through the acquisition of five additional companies. It gave me the chance to witness the transaction process as a buyer. Having sat on both sides of the table, I can tell you that Woodbridge is the finest M&A organization I have seen at work, as both a seller and a buyer.

As a customer, I can be very demanding and it is rare that I am completely satisfied by a vendor. I am fortunate to have enjoyed the finest vendor experience of my entire career during the most important transaction of my life—selling my business. Woodbridge International was transformational for me and I am confident their team can be for you, too! Congratulations on what you have built and good luck!

This book is designed to help you learn how best to sell your mid-size business in today's environment and how more buyers, more bids, higher price, and a better fit will lead to a successful close.

Mergers & Acquisitions Since 1993

Chapter 1

Introduction

By Don Krier, Senior Managing Director/Partner

Don Krier

We are writing this book after having been in the business of marketing and selling mid-size companies for over 31 years. The firm's seven partners: Robert Koenig, Don Krier, Larry Reinharz, Kyle Richard, Jacob Koenig, Simon Wibberley, and Marni Connelly, bring decades of experience from the mergers and acquisitions industry and are experts at running a confidential global auction process to help ensure our clients receive the highest value for their business.

We have the privilege and experience of working with entrepreneurs globally. We understand the mindset of the entrepreneur: Someone who has stepped out on his or her own, taken a risk, and built a business and made bold decisions. Now it is time to reap the rewards and sell the results of all the time, effort, and energy invested over the years.

You created something that did not exist before and have poured everything you have into it to make it work. There were no instruction manuals and lots of people may have told you it couldn't be done.

Against the odds, you succeeded.

Some may regard you as "lucky," but you know better than anyone that you make your own luck through hard work and avoiding the naysayers. You provide employment for people and put food on the table, shelter over the heads, and cars in the driveways for many families. Many people have come to rely on you.

At this point, it's time to think about the next move. It feels like the right time. The business is performing. You have navigated multiple obstacles over the years. Many a business owner has told us they are going to write a book to tell their stories. Now is the time to consider what is the best thing to do for the business, for yourself, and for your family.

We wrote this book because there isn't a one-size-fits-all answer. Selling your business may be a solution; however, it's not as straightforward as that.

The first questions we need to answer are: Why should you sell? What do you want to change or have life look like after the sale? Who should you use to help? And do all firms sell businesses the same way?

Different buyers will bring different solutions to the table, and their idea of the value of your business will vary accordingly. When it comes to the value of your company, beauty is in the eye of the beholder.

In this book, we cover the mechanics and other dynamics involved in the successful sale of your business. To start with, for a sale to succeed, you need to be:

1. Fully committed to selling:
   a. Mentally prepared with a sense of urgency to get it done
   b. Able to verbalize why you want to do this
   c. Able to verbalize why now
   d. Organized or willing to undertake getting your house in order
   e. Understand that time and surprises kill a deal
   f. Have the following in good order:
      i. Financial reporting
      ii. Operational and legal matters
      iii. A strong management team
2. Realistic about the value of your business
3. Clear about your vision for growth opportunities (your future story)
4. Forthright with all information because all successful deals are built on trust

Technological Advances and the Sale Process

Since our firm started in 1993, we have seen technology impact our practice and processes just as other businesses have been similarly impacted. We have embraced the change at every turn and have worked hard to improve our clients' experience while selling their companies. Technology is a critical component of our ability to create a great result for our clients. It enables us to fully educate them, provide them with multiple offers, and put them in control when selecting the ultimate buyer of their business. Embracing technology has allowed us to provide you with world-class research, create a competitive environment among buyers, and allowed us all to be much more efficient with your time.

For many years, the only way to really do extensive M&A industry and buyer research was to either have the resources of a Goldman Sachs, along with a back office of hundreds or thousands of researchers, or be an industry specialist and work very tightly within your given industry. The schools one attended or the fraternity or sorority you were a member of became sources of lifetime friends and one's first source for networking. Many bankers came into the investment banking world after having spent their early career building relationships and becoming an industry specialist.

We live in an entirely different world today, but many M&A firms and industry specialists sell companies in much the same way as they always have. Therefore, the old-fashioned legacy models of M&A no longer work. The old methodologies of finding buyers and completing transactions are as obsolete as the rotary phone and the Rolodex. We are competing with people who have done it the same way for 300 years. They are trained as analysts to go to the 50 to 100 "most likely" buyers.

Today's technology allows access to information like no other time in history. Yet, traditional M&A firms still do it the same way, even though new marketing and technology is available to improve the way it has always been done. Woodbridge thinking and methodology is radically different.

Industry Specialization Has Become Irrelevant

Industry specialists are struggling due to their very nature: They are caught in a time warp and not fully utilizing technology for the benefit of clients. No one can have a Rolodex as large as today's investment-oriented databases. More and more deals are completed not only between parties across the country but across the globe. Industry specialists simply do not think broadly enough to serve mid-size companies. There are tens of thousands of buyers able to acquire a company with $1 million to $20 million in EBITDA. Finding the perfect buyer who is sometimes an outlier cannot be achieved with a narrow list of industry buyers.

You have to think big, bold, and fearless to get a big price.

We once closed a transaction for an IT company that was first brought to market by an industry specialist. The industry specialist went to 60 buyers and could not get a deal completed. We marketed the company to more than 1,600 strategic buyers globally and 4,500 private equity firms and closed the deal for our client within our strict 150-day schedule.

Another seller recently engaged us after their former industry specialist went to 59 buyers, failed to generate interest, and gave up. In fact, several clients hire us each year after traditional firms fail to sell their business.

We continue to obtain more email addresses of potential buyers globally to expand our reach. We are driven to find more qualified buyers and look for the must-have buyer that sees the best fit.

As of this writing, we have built a global database of over 8,400 private-equity contacts. In addition, we have a proprietary, global database of over 420,000 email addresses of potential strategic buyers. And unlike anyone else in the industry, we create compelling marketing videos to showcase our client's business.

You are going to be reading about our two-day Management Meeting Training Workshop. Our clients attend class for two days of workshop training to prepare them for when they will be meeting with buyers. No one else in the industry takes the time we do to prepare you for that meeting with buyers. Our class is held virtually, as are all of the management meetings today. We want our clients going into this all-important meeting with buyers fully prepared and confident. The dress rehearsal is done and now it's showtime. You want to deliver your best, communicate the information buyers need to understand, and concisely articulate the future story of your company. We want the buyers coming out of that meeting saying, "I need to buy that company and raise my offer to get it!"

It's time to fully embrace new thinking and a better way to sell your business. The best marketing with the best team will find you the very best transaction. We *are* M&A.

We hope you find this book invaluable.

Chapter 2

Is Now the Time? And My Life After Closing

By Larry Reinharz, Senior Managing Director/Partner

WOODBRIDGE
International
Mergers & Acquisitions Since 1993

Larry Reinharz

Ideally, the best time to sell your company is when it's doing well and you don't have to sell. The wind is at your back, the outlook is robust, and somebody would ask, "Why the heck are you selling now?!"

Some reasons owners sell are: Waning enthusiasm for the company; the owner cannot bring the business to the next level, and believes it would be better off in the hands of a larger entity with more resources; the company has grown too fast and the owner "didn't sign up for this;" partnership disputes; health issues; and marital or family issues. And the biggest reason: You've got everything on the line every day. Stress. And you know good things don't last forever. So why not get out while things are good and smell the roses? Timing is everything.

Consider Amy's story:

Amy owned a growing $8 million consumer products business and was also the mother of two toddlers. Her business was well positioned. However, between raising her two children and giving attention to her third baby (her company) she felt spread too thin…something had to give! Her ideal buyer was someone who would free her up from the day-to-day responsibility of financing and running the business so she could focus on new product development and marketing. When she hired us, she felt it was a bit early, but better to be too early than too late!

Amy hired us a couple of months before the pandemic hit full force. Fortunately, her business actually benefited from the pandemic. We hit the market with her company in mid-April 2020—the peak of the pandemic! We did obtain multiple bidders, including a blue chip $19 billion private equity group that fell in love with Amy and were very excited to acquire her business as a platform company. It's highly unusual for a $19 billion fund to acquire an $8 million company as a platform; it speaks to the shortage of companies in the market—this fund had to dip down to deploy capital. Furthermore, we were able to negotiate a deal for Amy that was materially better than anticipated. Amy obtained her dream deal—she retained 30% of the company, and the private equity group freed her up from inside functions so she could focus on product development. Plus this group had an excellent track record of growing their platform companies so Amy was excited about her third baby's future.

The key is, Amy didn't hesitate…she felt it was maybe "too early," but unbeknownst to her or anyone, the timing was perfect—better to be too early than too late.

Unfortunately, we have too many opposite stories…business owners who delayed hiring us for months or years; the pandemic negatively impacted their companies; now their plans are on hold indefinitely.

Financial diversification is also a crucial factor in timing the sale of your company. Some entrepreneurs don't see their company as a risk since they created it and have a deep understanding of it. However, it is a financial asset subject to business cycles, competition, regulations, liability, and other uncertainties.

Many of our clients have the majority of their net worth tied up in their companies, and they need to view this as a concentrated financial position. Your risk profile is different when you are in your 20s, 30s, and 40s compared with 50 and older.

Here's Max's story:

I had been in touch with Max for eight years. Every year or so we'd get together and talk about his consumer products company and his challenges. He was growing the company very rapidly and obtaining strong profit margins. During an annual get-together he asked me about supply chain/logistics consultants to really move the needle on his business. Max felt he had to tighten up his supply chain, and he wasn't built that way—it didn't turn him on; he was more of a creative guy.

Sensing the business really didn't get his juices flowing anymore, he blurted out, "But I wouldn't sell the company now; the profits and outlook have never been better." I looked at him and he realized that's exactly the time to consider a sale. He asked me about a realistic value range and when I told him $20 million–$25 million, he almost fell off his chair.

We sold Max's company for $42 million; he obtained $37 million in cash and retained 10% of the company.

So the money made sense to him. He was only 42 years old, and he felt with that kind of money he'd have financial security for himself and his family and would have options to move on to other ventures. The business really didn't excite him anymore. He felt he had enhanced the business over the past 4–5 years, but now he was becoming more of a caretaker. Plus, as his company was growing, he realized the risks were also growing— knowing this wouldn't go on forever.

So the first step, once you've started thinking about selling, is understanding a realistic value range for your company. A business is a financial asset, so just like you might sell real estate, stocks, bonds, and other investments, you'd want to first understand a realistic price. After receiving our free value assessment, you then need to decide how meaningful those numbers are to you.

Everyone is different. In Max's case, if I had told him $10 million– $15 million, he would not have proceeded. Everyone has their number!

If you have the majority of your net worth in your company and you are past the 7th inning of your earning years, timing the sale is crucial to your financial well-being. The biggest mistake we've seen business owners make is waiting too long to sell. They do understand their company's value is tied to profitability and growth and are bullish on the future…but they're waiting for the "peak." Based on our experience, if you find the "peak," by then it's too late! The business has peaked and is now declining…and nobody wants to catch a falling knife.

This next story also demonstrates that point:

> A family healthcare staffing business engaged us to sell their company. We obtained real bids in the value range we quoted up front: $8 million–$12 million. They felt the business had more upside and put their plans to sell on hold. A couple of years later, the market completely shifted and their volume dropped by 65%. The family wanted to re-engage us to sell the business; however, it was now worth $2 million–$3 million, actually too small for us to pursue—not to mention at that level it didn't make financial sense for them to sell.

> Brian and Michael were partners in a finance business and wanted to sell all or a majority of the company to capitalize on its upward trends. We went to market and obtained offers in the $10 million–$15 million range, which confirmed the range we gave them prior to engagement. Michael convinced Brian that the outlook for their business was too good to sell now for this amount of money, so they decided to hold onto the business. Just a year later, the market completely changed and they had to liquidate the business, walking away with approximately $3 million.

Somebody once asked Andrew Carnegie how he accumulated all of his wealth and he said, "I always sold too soon."

It's better to be too early than too late on timing the sale of your business.

Your Life After Closing

Deciding when to sell also involves envisioning life after the sale. Once you transition out of your company, how will you spend your time? Typically, the transition period is anywhere from six to 18 months. You may think obtaining $10 million, $20 million, $30 million or whatever your number is will solve all of your problems, but it only solves your money problems.

For most business owners we speak with, thinking about their life after closing is the most challenging discussion we have, and it has many different dimensions. The financial aspect is fairly simple: We discuss realistic ranges, we go to market, meet or exceed their expectations, and then they're ready to go, right? Not necessarily.

Here's one actual example:

> Dr. A had a medical practice in the Southwest. We provided him with a realistic value range of $20 million–$25 million. He was fine with that, hired us, and we went to market. We did significantly better than our original value estimate: Offers came in closer to $30 million. He suddenly went silent, and we couldn't get him on the telephone. Finally, he resurfaced after a couple of weeks. "I thought about this," he said. "I'm 46 years old—if my wife and I spend more than five hours together daily, we'll end up getting a divorce!"

When qualifying prospective clients, I ask them to articulate how they'll spend their time after transitioning out of the business.

I've also heard, "Believe me, I'd love to have the problem of doing nothing." True, many of our clients have dealt with the daily grind for a long time: Sleepless nights, struggling to make payroll, staying ahead of the competition, personally guaranteeing debt. Being a successful business owner is all-consuming, and it's difficult to fully detach.

So while the dream of just "playing" is appealing, how long can you play or enjoy leisure time until you start getting antsy—or until your spouse kicks you out of the house? Our clients who have thought through these scenarios have the least amount of seller's remorse or general stress during the process of selling their "baby." Some of them determine what their Life After Closing will look like by discussing with family, friends, trusted advisors, therapists, financial advisors, lawyers—and Woodbridge.

At the end of the day, the business owner will recognize they will have freedom after selling their business and the ability to move on to the next chapter.

Chapter 3

What Is My Business Worth?

By Don Krier, Senior Managing Director/Partner

WOODBRIDGE
International
Mergers & Acquisitions Since 1993

Don Krier

One of the first questions we are often asked is: "Can you tell me what you believe my business is worth?"

Having represented clients and selling companies since 1993, one thing that I can promise you is that no two offers will be the same. Every buyer will look at your business differently—each brings their own set of value and opportunity to the business. I always tell business owners that beauty is in the eye of the beholder. Value depends on the new owner's vision of what they can do with the business going forward. All your trends will be important: Revenue, EBITDA, position in the industry, strength of the management team; however, most importantly: Where can the business go and what does the buyer bring to take it into the future?

Because we have sold so many businesses, we have a great understanding of how buyers think and how they value businesses. In 2023, we averaged 21 bids per company that we sold. In the first quarter of 2023, we set a company record having generated 62 bids on a company we brought to market. We receive several hundred bids over the course of a year and hear what questions buyers are asking.

How Buyers Think

There is a strategy you will see buyers often use when looking at a business. They will spend a lot of time studying all the historical information about your company. In fact, they will discuss the past performance of the business while all the time looking for opportunities to expand and grow the business in the future. If a buyer can't clearly see how to grow the business, they are not goingto buy the business.

The premium buyer is the one who has fully recognized their opportunity to bring something to the transaction that is new or different to enhance the business. There are a multitude of things that can be done, and they will vary with each buyer:

- Cross-selling to your customers
- Finding new sourcing for products or for manufacturing/distribution
- Acquiring or developing new technologies/patents
- Reducing manufacturing time/costs
- Increasing marketing expenditures to boost overall sales
- Opening a new market in a new country (we have done a number of transactions where a foreign buyer was making their first entry to the U.S. market)
- Broadening a product line
- Acquiring new personnel/talent
- Increasing market share
- Improving systems and business reporting/controls

It is not uncommon for us to receive 20–40 written offers on a company that we bring to market. The offers will vary, and the highest offer can be twice the value of the lowest one. **Again, beauty is in the eye of the beholder.**

Reality Check

It's a waste of everyone's time to take a company to market with unrealistic value expectations. Our objective is to give you a range of value that we feel confident of hitting with the odds in the 80%–90% range. If the gap is too large between what you want for your business and what we believe is realistic or possible, we will advise not taking the company to market at this time. We will instead suggest ways to improve the business, including finding ways to:

Become more profitable, grow your business, increase margins, reduce overhead, increase marketing, find new customers, etc.

So, what do we look for in a company to determine value?

- **Customer base**
  - Percentage of revenue derived from each of your top 5 customers
  - Customer longevity/turnover
  - Recurring revenue from customers
  - Any spikes that have occurred in revenue that may or may not be sustainable. We saw this frequently during the pandemic.
- **Products and services**
  - Do you manufacture or exclusively distribute the product?
  - Do you own patents?
  - Why do customers do business with you?
  - What are your competitive advantages?
- **Market share**
  - Market size and percentage of market share the company has
  - How is the market changing, for better or worse?
  - Where will this market be in 5 years? 10 years?
- **Growth opportunities**
  - Product and service mix, extensions or diversification
  - New geographic markets
  - New verticals/industries to pursue
- **Depth of management**
  - Are the right people in place to take the business to the next level?
  - How long will you stay?
  - Are all your critical functional areas staffed adequately?
  - Do you have too many employees?
  - Culture and benefits

- **Financials**
  - Working capital required presently and for the future
  - Capital expenditure requirements—short term and long term
  - Quality of systems for financial reporting:
    - Financials—audited, reviewed or compiled?
    - Ability to produce monthly financials
  - Inventory quality and levels
  - Track record:
    - Sales and recast EBITDA history and outlook
    - Growth rates
    - Gross profit margin history
- **Ownership**
  - Number of owners and percentages of ownership (i.e. how many decision makers?)
  - Motivation of the ownership for a transaction—what is the end game?
- **Technology**
  - Is the company on the cutting edge of technology in its field?
  - How has technology affected the industry and how will it affect the company in the future?
- **Facility**
  - Own or lease?
  - Capacity within the existing facility
- **Quality of earnings (Q of E)**
  This topic will be covered in later chapters. Quality of earnings has an impact on value in terms of the risk a buyer feels they are taking, evaluating ratios, recurring revenue streams, and future outlook—for the industry, the products, the technology, etc.

Avoid Comparing Yourself to Others

One of the mistakes we often see is a business owner comparing their company to another company recently sold, which is "just like our business." Over the years we've observed this to be a deadly trap, as no two businesses are the same.

While from the outside companies can look the same, beyond that point they can vary dramatically. I have lifted the hood on hundreds of companies over the years and can assure you that no two companies are the same and hence the value will in fact be different.

We have sold companies for 4x recast EBITDA through 15x EBITDA, as well as for 50% of revenue and 700% of revenue, and others for simply the asset value. While the history of the company is important, where the company is positioned to go into the future is even more important. Buyers are buying the future.

We will work with you to capture the future story of your business!

Chapter 4

Now Is the Time – What Should I Do to Prepare My Company for Sale?

By Larry Reinharz, Senior Managing Director/Partner

WOODBRIDGE
International
Mergers & Acquisitions Since 1993

Larry Reinharz

In our experience, the best time to sell your company is when these four conditions have been met:

- Your EBITDA is trending at a level that will realistically provide you with the price you desire
- The six to 12-month outlook for the business is strong
- You are mentally prepared to pull the trigger if you are offered your price
- The macro environment is favorable

So what should you do now?

1. **Keep nurturing and fostering your Golden Goose.**
   With Woodbridge, from start to finish, selling a company is a 150-day process. The most important thing is to stay focused on business performance. Keep up the sense of urgency. Continue reinvesting for the future. In short, continue to do all the things that have made your company successful—and act like you're not selling the company!

   Don't take your foot off the gas pedal, because if you do, the operation or its pipeline will decline, and your deal could get renegotiated; or, the buyer may get spooked and walk away. **The No. 1 reason our deals die or get delayed is declining financial performance, so keep the pedal to the metal!**

   You've been successful at making prudent investments and exploiting opportunities. Over the years some worked and some didn't, but on balance you've made good decisions that have paid off…so keep doing that and trust your judgment. Don't feel you have to hold back or keep a particular buyer in mind while making investment decisions.

The fact is that each interested buyer will have their own angle on how they feel they can grow your company. Stick with basic attributes that have made you successful: growth, profitability, turnkey operations, motivated staff, and proprietary products, services, and technologies. In other words, constant improvement of the business. Plus, at the end of the day, if for some reason the sale doesn't go through, you've kept the business vibrant and growing and haven't missed a beat.

Cost-cutting and EBITDA when preparing to sell

Some business owners start micromanaging the EBITDA while losing sight of the big picture. Most buyers will express their valuations as a multiple of trailing 12 months adjusted EBITDA. Consequently, many owners start digging into their expenses and questioning whether or not the new buyer really "needs" marketing, sales, administrative, labor, etc.

Think about it: "I save $100,000 in expenses and sell at 6x EBITDA; that's $600,000 more I just put in my pocket!" This is not to say you shouldn't eliminate fat. Every owner understands where there are excessive or unnecessary expenses in their company. So, wherever there is fat, make the tough decision and cut it now. This way you've proven it really was unnecessary.

It's more impactful to make the cut as you prepare to sell rather than explaining later to a buyer, "Well, you really don't need this person or service." Assume buyers are from Missouri: Show me.

You don't want to kill the Golden Goose! Eliminating investments that have kept your company growing and vibrant will decrease the value of the company...so stick to the instincts that have made you successful up to now.

Accurate & Timely Financial Statements

Having accurate and timely financial statements is crucial in getting a deal done for maximum value.

The story of a former client illustrates this point: A manufacturer we sold recently had a difficult time submitting timely financial information, which created a six-week delay in getting the business to market. Eventually we did get his business to market and obtained 10 offers for the company, ranging from $6 million–$12 million; our client signed a letter of intent (LOI) with the strongest buyer for $12 million in cash. About one month after signing the LOI, our client lost his biggest customer, reducing EBITDA from $2 million to a break-even.

Unfortunately, he was also personally guaranteeing $5 million of debt and the banks were getting concerned. His loans ended up in the "problem area," and he was spending his time fielding calls from bank lawyers. After exhausting all lender take-out possibilities, we found him a strategic buyer who wanted his capacity and geography. So the deal our client obtained was $6 million in cash and the potential to earn another $6 million over the next several years based on performance. After paying off debt and closing costs, our client walked away with $300,000 in cash instead of the $6 million in cash he would have obtained had he provided timely financial statements. **A six-week delay cost him nearly all his liquidity.**

The good news is that accurate and timely financial statements are something you can obtain. For some of you it will take more time and money than others, but it can be done and is crucial to getting a deal done for maximum value.

Imagine how our client felt losing all his liquidity because he could not supply us with timely and accurate financial statements! One way you can assess the quality of your financial statements is to share them with us and we'll let you know how good they are. Depending on your situation we may be able to work with what you have, or refer you to CPA firms or part-time CFOs we work with throughout North America.

2. **Continue to work yourself out of a job.** This seems to be the biggest leap for entrepreneurs to take. It's difficult to delegate and let go of your "baby." At a minimum, you should evolve out of being directly responsible for incoming or new business—the less, the better. Focus on transitioning any customer or client relationships to employees. If you don't currently have the in-house talent for this role and staff that you can trust, look to hire someone. Ideally, the company is firing on all cylinders and you are truly a chairman operating at a high level. You are not going into the office often, and your involvement is primarily attending quarterly board meetings or monthly review of financial results and outlook. We've completed deals for both extremes, and the chairman-level business owner will obtain 35%–75% more cash when the deal closes.

   A quick story:

   David hired us to sell his growing e-commerce business, and we both felt the business would sell for approximately $25 million. After attending our two-day Management Meeting Training, David was convinced that hiring a strong executive behind him would provide buyers with more comfort. Prior to approaching buyers, he brought on a strong #2 and was transparent with that person on his objectives. The #2 attended buyer meetings with David and presented the growth opportunities to the buyers. Ultimately, we sold the business for $35 million, and David's #2 negotiated his compensation package—including ownership in the business—with the buyer directly.

3. **Negative Surprises in Due Diligence.** Disclose, disclose, disclose! Buyers will find any skeletons or issues. If you fail to disclose something material and the buyer finds it on their own, there's a breakdown in trust and credibility. The buyer will wonder, "What else are they not disclosing?"

If there's a lack of trust, it becomes very difficult to complete a transaction.

You know all the issues with your business and personal history. You know where the skeletons are, so disclose everything up front with the Woodbridge underwriting team: previous, current or pending litigation, penalties, fines, tax issues, prior bankruptcies, labor issues…anything you feel is a negative. Bring it up during the first discussion with the Woodbridge underwriting team. Believe me, we've seen it all!

Whatever you feel is an issue may not be a major issue, and if it is we will put a game plan in motion to either rectify it or disclose it at a certain point in the deal process. Just like timely and accurate financial statements, transparency and full disclosure are achievable, and should be addressed before your business goes to market. Nearly all issues can be fixed; it's just a question of time and money.

A quick story on full disclosure:

We were selling a distribution company with about $20 million in revenue. The owners told us their salespeople were all W-2 employees. We ran a successful auction and our clients signed a letter of intent with a very capable strategic buyer with a value that exceeded our client's expectations. When the buyer went into due diligence, they discovered that the salespeople were all 1099 independent contractors, not W-2 employees. Honestly, not a big deal, but our client knew the difference between independent contractors and W-2 employees, so why did they lie? And if they lied about this simple thing, what else would they be lying about? The buyers walked and the deal died.

Trust is the most important factor in completing deals… without trust, a deal won't get done.

Chapter 5

Time Is of the Essence & DealRoom

By CJ Perrone, Vice President/Closing

WOODBRIDGE
International
Mergers & Acquisitions Since 1993

CJ Perrone

When you engage Woodbridge, selling your business is a 150-day process. If things happen to derail or delay the process, risk of your deal not closing increases.

The process run by a typical investment banker relies on a small group of unspecialized individuals for every deal facet—Woodbridge leverages teams dedicated to their specific craft within our process (e.g., research, marketing, closing). As a result, our methods drive deals to close in an average of 67 days where a traditional investment bank can take anywhere from nine months to years. A philosophy of less time, fewer roadblocks and no surprises yields a simple result: selling your business with a high degree of certainty to close.

How has Woodbridge managed to set an industry standard with our selling process? Two key tenets: 1) Our philosophy of accountability and discipline and 2) our mechanization of the M&A process.

An integral part of moving quickly in a deal is driving accountability and discipline across all parties involved (e.g., ourselves, our clients, our buyers, and third parties involved in the transaction). All parties must feel the urgency of the deal, and that starts with knowing exactly what needs to be done and when it needs to be done by— we are running an auction with consequences if a potential buyer does not meet expectations.

Without a well-defined timeline, "deal drag" or unexpected delays are inevitable.

With this understanding in mind, Woodbridge has invested countless hours and significant dollars to build a process with a project-management-focused mentality. At any given moment in our process, all parties know exactly what is on their plate and are expected to adhere to our timeline.

To accomplish this, we utilize a combination project management solution and virtual data room ("VDR") called DealRoom. DealRoom allows us to implement the same tried-and-true process across all deals to achieve ultimate visibility and accountability in all of our transactions. Some high-level features of the platform, which actively contribute to minimizing the time it takes to get deals done include:

- Assignment of tasks within our process (e.g., diligence items, requests for information, etc.)
- Creation of a schedule of task-based due dates with visual Gantt charts
- Progress monitoring of every task necessary to move the deal along
- Activity monitoring of every involved party and their assigned tasks/documents necessary to move the deal along

This process is only as urgent and accountable as the people who are involved, and that includes the Seller. Preparation and a proactive mindset are key—the concept of pay me now or pay me later holds true in the M&A process. Woodbridge and our clients have found the most successful transactions are ones where robust preparation, including the build-out of a premarket VDR, is undergone. Sophisticated buyers will put a target acquisition under a level of scrutiny likely not experienced by the business owner—they want to know exactly what they are buying and minimize their investment risk. Sellers who do not put the preparation in ahead of when our process expects to begin receiving letters of intent from buyers have immediately disadvantaged themselves. Sellers who embrace Woodbridge's process and follow our published process in DealRoom find themselves having anywhere between 35% and 45% of a buyer's due diligence requests complete before an LOI is even received, thus shaving weeks off of a more "traditional" close process.

Time Kills Deals

Business owners choose to sell their companies when the timing is right. The longer a process takes, the more likely something will occur that will cause the "right time" to go wrong. We've seen this occur more times than one would imagine—and always to the disadvantage of the business owner. The lesson: "Strike while the iron is hot."

Time kills deals due to many different factors. If trends in a business go negative, buyers will become far more conservative in their approach. Buyers do not like to purchase businesses with negative trends unless they can get them extremely cheap, for obvious reasons.

Sell when trends are positive and close before they have a chance to turn against you.

The longer a sale process goes on, the more likely it is that extraneous factors can affect the business or adversely impact the sale process. All it takes is a hurricane, a recession, a terrorist attack, a stock market correction, a crucial employee with a sudden health issue, a lost customer, a product issue or a lawsuit to sabotage the momentum of a sale process that is moving in the right direction.

Think about it: If the macro environment is right, if your business is trending well, and your EBITDA is at a level that gives you the value you want, you should sell it today. If you wait too long, many factors can impact the situation.

Elements of Our 150-Day Timeline

The timeline for selling your company has three main parts:

1. Underwriting, preparation of marketing materials and buyer research—45 days
2. Marketing campaign and buyer selection—45 days
3. Buyer due diligence/closing—60 days

We will delve into the activities involved in these three phases in the coming chapters.

Chapter 6

Presenting My Company to the Market

How to Position My Company for Sale

By Priscilla Schmieder, Vice President
Financial Analysis & Client Marketing Materials

By Priscilla Schmieder

Imagine a well-funded buyer with plenty of investment opportunities to choose from, such as growing their own business organically or acquiring any other company in the market. What makes YOUR business so special that they should pause to consider it?

Ideally, your company will be "packaged" for sale as a unique investment opportunity with a superb return. Buyers will be laser-focused on your growth story, because that is what will make the business worth more in the future.

Some entrepreneurs choose to run their businesses at stable performance, which is absolutely fine and easily understood— there are plenty of reasons for this choice. Even if this is your case, imagine a buyer with the motivation and resources to radically grow your company. How far could they grow in 2-5 years? How big is the market and what share of it do you have today? Why is your company uniquely positioned to capture more? Which route should be taken to reach this ambitious goal? Is your business scalable? How much will they have to spend on resources (e.g., new hires, equipment, physical space)?

After the growth outlook is understood, a series of risk-related questions come up: Will people still need your company's products or services 20 years from now? What happens if you lose your largest customer? How does your business hold up during a recession? What about a pandemic? Does your business depend on any individual suppliers? How threatening is the competition? How easy is it for new entrants to compete with you?

These are questions answered by the materials that Woodbridge creates to take its clients to market.

Teaser: The Hook

The teaser is a one-page executive summary describing your business, with:

- Key financials and projections
- A concise description of products or services and customer base
- Future growth story
- Reasons the business is sustainable and defensible against competitors

The teaser omits your company's name, exact location, and other identifying features. This allows you to send it out to as many potential buyers as you like. Woodbridge sends teasers to thousands of recipients at a time, as you will see in the next chapter of this book.

The purpose of the teaser is to attract buyers' attention and create interest in your company. An effective teaser:

1. **Breaks through the noise.** Most buyers of middle-market companies see dozens of potential acquisitions every week; this is especially true of financial buyers (private equity groups). You have one page to capture attention and elicit initial interest. The headline and subject line of the email need to be attention-grabbing: Headline-worthy features include high margins, double-digit growth, proprietary assets and market leadership.

2. **Creates excitement with a story of vast future growth.** How big is the market? What share of it do you have today? How could you double or triple your revenue or EBITDA? Would you hire salespeople? Open new locations? Develop new products or services? Add capacity?

CIM: Information Driving Bids

After buyers sign a Non-Disclosure Agreement (NDA) to learn more, they receive a Confidential Information Memorandum (CIM, or "the book"). This "book" should contain enough information and plenty of reasons for them to bid on your business. It includes an overview of:

- Product/Service Mix
- Customer Base
- Sales & Marketing
- Operations
- Suppliers
- Facilities
- IT and Equipment
- Organization/HR
- Financial Statements & Projections

The CIM needs to contain sufficient information for buyers to decide to bid, without going overboard on details. Our experience shows that when there is excessive information, readers either don't notice key messages or just stop reading altogether.

In the M&A market, books are typically written by financial analysts. At Woodbridge, we take a different approach. We have business writers working with financial analysts to create each CIM. This combined talent tells each company's distinctive story and positions it for greatest interest, while accurately explaining financial performance and presenting solid, defensible forecasts.

The Movie: Your Business Featured in a Two-Minute Video

Adding a professionally produced video to your written materials sets your company apart from the other deals that buyers see every day. Sure, buyers want to see your financial performance, customer base, target markets and infrastructure, but a quick visual "visit" to your company makes an instant impression.

Buyers receiving Woodbridge books and videos have commented on the outstanding quality of both, and are particularly engaged by the marketing video we create for every seller. After signing a Confidentiality Agreement (or NDA), the buyer receives the book and video link and is able to watch the owner discuss some of the highlights of his or her business, as well as get a peek into how things run, the facility, and general atmosphere.

You can watch dozens of marketing videos on Woodbridge's Deals Done page. You'll notice that engaging marketing videos can be produced for every type of industry.

Chapter 7

Creating a Competitive Auction: Broad vs. Narrow Marketing

By Marni Connelly, Managing Director/Partner – COO

WOODBRIDGE
International
Mergers & Acquisitions Since 1993

Marni Connelly

Research and Marketing

- How do you create a robust list of potential buyers for your business?
- How do you quickly and strategically get those groups involved in an auction process?
- How do you receive the most bids for your business?
- How do you receive the best bids?
- How can you be sure you have found the best buyer and offer?
- Can you really sell your business to a global buyer?
- How do you increase your certainty to close?

Marketing your business requires an integrated, global approach that utilizes industry insight, innovative tools, and proven tactics that move buyers to closing. At Woodbridge International, our approach is to cast a wide net to uncover hidden opportunities that others miss. This net is centered on your industry, but vast enough to include related industries, generating the broadest possible exposure for your business and reaching the largest pool of qualified potential buyers.

Woodbridge's marketing reaches buyers you might not have thought of or even be familiar with. For example, international buyers actively seek acquisitions in North America to enter the world's largest market.

The key to obtaining the best offers for your business is keeping prospective buyers engaged. Woodbridge's process instills in them a sense of urgency and a reason to adhere to our 150-day timeline. This tactic, combined with extensive outreach, attracts the most qualified potential buyers—those who are often not the most obvious at the outset.

Getting more offers allows you to find not only the best buyer but also the one with the best fit and highest certainty to close.

Marketing Like No One Else

Woodbridge International has developed a proprietary database of 8,400 private equity groups with approximately 5,200 located in North America. All of them are approached, in addition to 4,000–10,000 strategic buyers selected according to our client's business.

It is impossible to think one can predetermine the best buyers and capture them all in a potential buyer list of 50–100 targets, which is how a traditional investment bank approaches marketing. In each industry, there are thousands of companies capable of buying a middle-market company. Strategic and financial buyers constantly change strategy and focus, so even if you spoke to a particular company recently and they had no acquisition plans, they could now be interested in acquisitions due to a new CEO, recent funding, or a change in strategy.

Woodbridge has completed many successful transactions where the selected buyer who completed the deal was not an obvious buyer, and therefore a traditional firm would not have contacted them. These include cross-border buyers, related-industry buyers, and private equity groups.

Your business will also be promoted confidentially on the Engagements page of our website and online at well-known trade sites. You will review the teaser and all other marketing materials prior to going to market.

How do we create the global marketing list?
Research, research, research.

Formulating a marketing plan and reaching prospective buyers is a multilayered process. The focus is on demand generation supported by a dedicated research team. We develop the marketing list based on thorough discussions with our clients, combined with database searches and examining M&A transactions in their industry to pick up on any companies that are doing acquisitions.

Our marketing teams are skilled at unveiling the best buyer for your business, with the most attractive terms and the greatest certainty to close.

Through a collaborative process to create the most comprehensive list, some of the questions we ask our clients are:

- Who are your competitors, customers, and suppliers?
- Do you attend or know of any prominent trade shows or journals in your industry?
- Have any companies ever approached you to sell?
- Who would you consider to be an ideal buyer of your company?

Our marketing list is created using a proprietary database we have built over the last 31 years that covers the entire globe, as well as a variety of "gold standard" investment banking databases. Our search criteria utilize industry classifications, keywords, revenue size, and geography for direct competitors as well as for those in related industries. We also use specialized lists, such as businesses owned by indigenous North American people, franchisors, and top-100 rankings.

We develop a buyer list that contains approximately 15,000 strategic and financial buyers globally and hit this list multiple times via a combination of emails and calls.

Ready to Go to Market

After the blind executive summary (teaser) has been approved, the campaign begins.

Woodbridge marketing has honed its email automation process over several years. Each campaign comprises multiple sends in a cadence of proven effectiveness. Campaigns are dynamic, with subject lines, teasers, and recipient lists adjusted according to open rates, click-through rates and even the profile of engaged parties. In addition, we often conduct A/B testing of teasers prior to full-scale launch and create customized versions for specific segments.

Teaser recipients who are interested in learning more about your company will request and sign a non-disclosure agreement (NDA) before release of the Company Information Memorandum (CIM, or "book") and marketing video.

All strategic buyers will be vetted to assess their qualifications and passed by you for approval as their interest comes in. This is all before the book and video is released, which is the first time they will learn your company's name.

Strategic vs. Financial Buyers

What is a strategic buyer? Strategic buyers in your industry or related industries will often look for companies to fill a certain need or create synergy within their existing business or business units. These types of buyers can include competitors, suppliers, and customers.

An example of a potential strategic buyer that comes from related industries would be if a supply-chain management and logistics company bought a food manufacturer. Other buyers might be looking to enter a particular market segment, often the case with regional, national or global cross-border deals. For them, purchasing an existing company in a new market is more cost-effective than starting from scratch.

What is a financial buyer? Financial buyers include private equity groups (PEGs), family funds, and search funds.

If your business is considered by a PEG as an add-on, synergies and fit with their existing company will be key to their investment decision. If it is being considered as a platform, your growth story will have greater importance. Post-acquisition, platform investments typically receive more direct oversight from PEGs, while add-ons are likely to have more interaction with their parent companies.

PEGs that specialize in acquiring companies in the middle-market space will often take an active role from a board level providing financial acumen, talent, and strategy to reach the next level of growth and raise its market value. PEGs generally acquire businesses with the goal of selling them after 5–7 years.

Who is the obvious buyer? Obvious buyers are companies we are often most familiar with. But this alone does not make them the best buyer. With our approach, 75% of the time our clients are bought by someone they had never heard of.

This is the importance of going to market with an open mind and no assumptions. Timing is everything. At any moment your company could be the latest strategic vision for a buyer.

Your Marketing Advocate

After interested parties sign an NDA, they become "book holders." Woodbridge International Marketing Associates contact each one during the campaign to ensure they have received the book, read it, and watched the video. They'll answer questions and share positive updates about your company each week. The Marketing Associate's primary purpose is to get as many book holders to issue bids during the 21-day bid acceptance period as possible.

Marketing associates also provide our clients with a weekly campaign status report and call. A campaign status report typically includes the following information on leads:

- **Book holders:** Potential buyers who have the book and video
- **Book-pass:** Book holders who have declined to pursue the opportunity

- **Engaged Groups:** Book holders who are asking additional questions and/or requesting additional information
- **Book-bid:** Potential buyers who have placed an LOI or non-binding valuation offer

Woodbridge's expert, highly trained Marketing Associates advocate on your company's behalf and are tenacious in the pursuit of the most attractive bids for your business. Not only do they generate significant interest and persuade people to make a bid, they expedite the entire sales process.

It's this type of advocacy combined with personalized attention to your deal that gives your business significant advantage over the thousands of other deals on the market.

After receipt of all bids, the Closing team will then put together a bid comparison summary and decide with you who should come into Management Meetings.

Here's an example of how marketing makes the difference:

The owner of a $20-million distribution business hired us to market his company. He already had a $12 million offer in hand from a capable strategic buyer but felt the $8 million cash portion of the offer was too low. We went to market and obtained 23 other bids for the company. His existing buyer stayed in the process and increased their bid to $13 million, all cash. Nice, right? Not nice enough—our client ended up selling to another buyer for $16 million, all cash!

Confidentially Market to a Large Number of Buyers Globally

 More Buyers

 More Bids

 Higher Price

 Better Fit

Related Industries
4,388

Core Industry Buyers
2,925

Foreign Industry Players
2,406

Client-Known Buyers
25

Private Equity Groups
8,411

Traditional
M&A
Goes to
Client-Known
Buyers
50–100

Woodbridge International

Total: 18,130

**Average for last
5 deals in market
in 2023**

75% of the Time, the Buyer Was Not Previously Known to Our Client

Chapter 8

Calculating Adjusted EBITDA and Getting Through Due Diligence

By Kyle Richard, Managing Partner

Kyle Richard

- What is EBITDA?
- What should you expect when due diligence starts?
- What can you do to prepare for due diligence?

The first step is getting your numbers in order. The second step is gathering the proper information to substantiate your key business relationships and financial results, and the third step is to identify the perceived risks to a buyer that are inherent to your business. Mitigating these risks as best you can ahead of time will enable you to get through due diligence in a timely manner.

In this chapter, you will learn:

- What EBITDA is, why it is important, and how to calculate it
- How to define working capital and why you should pay attention to it
- What to expect during the due diligence process

EBITDA—the Holy Grail of Valuation

EBITDA is the most widely used calculation for determining valuation in the middle-market space. It quantifies the ongoing cash flows available to the owner of a company. Financial and strategic buyers will typically use an EBITDA figure to determine what your company is worth to them. The acronym EBITDA refers to the company's annual Earnings Before Interest, Taxes (income taxes), Depreciation, and Amortization. The calculation has become widely used in middle-market M&A because it:

- Eliminates the impact of financing on your existing capital structure by adding back interest expenses
- Eliminates the impact of your existing entity structure by adding back income taxes

- Quantifies the real cash flow of an organization by adding back depreciation and amortization (non-cash expenses)
- Determines the real cash flow of an organization by adding back depreciation and amortization (non-cash expenses)

The EBITDA calculation allows a potential buyer to assess an acquisition candidate's cash flow by layering in their own desired capital and tax structure.

EBITDA should be calculated using financial results on an accrual basis and not on a cash basis. Furthermore, EBITDA should be based on financial data that follows Generally Accepted Accounting Principles (GAAP). By reporting in accordance with GAAP, your company's financial results can be interpreted and understood by potential buyers around the world.

Unadjusted vs. Adjusted EBITDA

Certain adjustments must be made to EBITDA to determine the true ongoing cash flows that will be enjoyed by the buyer of the company. This means EBITDA should be adjusted using two types of addbacks: (1) discretionary expenses and (2) non-recurring items. Each adjustment type is described below.

Discretionary Expenses

If you're like most middle-market business owners, you probably have "tax-incentivized" expenses running through your books, i.e., personal or owner discretionary expenses. By adjusting EBITDA, you get the opportunity to add back to EBITDA the perks you have been receiving over time that were actually profits of the company. These adjustments represent expenses that are not ordinary, necessary or prudent to perpetuate business operations and will not continue under new ownership. Types of examples for positive addbacks to EBITDA include the following:

- Compensation paid over fair market value to owner-operators
- Personal telephone or other utility expenses

- Personal residence bills paid by the company
- Owner's hobbies that are paid for by the company
- Above-market rent paid to a related party
- Salaries or benefits paid to/for non-working friends/family
- Owner life insurance premiums
- Over/under arm's-length transactions to related parties
- Personal auto expenses
- Non-business meals and entertainment
- Golf memberships paid for by owner
- Charity or gifts paid for by the company

Personal or discretionary benefits might also have a downward or negative impact on cash flow. These must also be considered in an adjusted EBITDA calculation. Common examples include:

- Compensation paid under fair market value to owner-operators
- Replacement salary of an owner-operator or lack of a key executive that is needed such as a CFO
- Below-market rent paid by the company
- Over/under arm's-length transactions to related parties

Non-Recurring Items

One-time or non-recurring expenses should be added back to EBITDA to normalize cash flow, so that cash flow reflects what a buyer will experience in the future. A non-recurring expense is an activity or event that took place during a particular period and is not expected to occur again; i.e., it was abnormal in nature. Adding back these expenses may result in upward or downward adjustments to your EBITDA analysis. Some examples of non-recurring expenses are:

- Legal fees and litigation expenses
- Consulting fees
- One-time repairs

- Fines
- Business relocation costs
- Lease-breaking fee
- Plant/branch shutdown costs
- Costs to rebrand
- Software upgrade

Profit & Loss Statement—EBITDA Calculation

XYZ Company, Inc   **Exhibit A**

	201X
Income	$40,000,000
Less: Cost of Goods Sold	25,000,000
Gross Profit	15,000,000
Expenses	
Salaries & Wages	5,500,000
Rent	250,000
Professional Fees	800,000
Travel & Entertainment	450,000
Auto Expense	200,000
Telephone & Utilities	120,000
Advertising, Marketing & Promotion	200,000
Repairs & Maintenance	150,000
Insurance	180,000
Taxes	150,000
Depreciation	200,000
Amortization	50,000
Interest	100,000
Total Expenses	8,350,000
Net Income from Operations	6,650,000
Add Back	
Interest	100,000
Taxes	150,000
Depreciation	200,000
Amortization	50,000
EBITDA	$7,150,000

Profit & Loss Statement

EBITDA Calculation

Once your company's earnings have been reviewed for adjustments, a normalized EBITDA analysis may look like this:

During the deal process, it is essential to demonstrate to a buyer what the recurring cash flows of your company were historically and what they will continue to be into the future. For a company with significant capital expenditures, a buyer will also look at annual normalized capital expenditures when determining cash flows.

The Importance of the Balance Sheet and Working Capital

EBITDA is not the only important calculation in a middle-market M&A deal. A buyer will require a seller to deliver the company with a sufficient level of working capital to operate the company properly. The rationale for this is that the buyer should not have to put additional working capital into the company immediately after purchase, and should not be able to pull working capital out of the company immediately after purchase.

Working capital is current assets less current liabilities and is normally calculated on a cash-free, debt-free basis. You should analyze your balance sheet critically to determine whether assets and liabilities are fairly stated, and to ensure that any contingent assets and liabilities are captured.

Typical questioned due diligence items include the collectability of aged accounts receivable, valuation and/or obsolescence of inventory, quantification of prepaid assets, and articulation of why aged accounts payable are outstanding. If there is opportunity to lower the level of required inventory or improve the collection time with accounts receivable, this should be undertaken prior to selling your business.

What to Expect—Confirmatory Due Diligence

While no two deals are exactly alike, the confirmatory due diligence phase of a deal generally starts when a letter of intent (LOI) has been signed and exclusivity granted to a single buyer.

Before exclusivity, a buyer will likely do their own diligence assessments by reviewing the data room, meeting management, industry/market research, and asking questions. However, usually within a couple of days of a signed LOI, you should expect a buyer to engage third-party professionals to perform an in-depth diligence assessment of your company.

In most cases, an accounting or financial firm will perform a Quality of Earnings analysis (or financial diligence), a law firm will conduct an in-depth legal review and the buyer will review all operations in detail. The buyer will also engage other outside firms to conduct due diligence, which may include specialists in taxes, insurance, HR, environmental, plant operations, and market studies.

Generally, each of these projects begins with a conference call to introduce all parties, after which the relevant parties are given access to the data room and field visits are scheduled.

The scope, size, and complexity of each diligence assignment differs in importance as a function of the buyer's risk appetite, but in each case the overall diligence assessment will be a thorough review of all aspects of the business. Every diligence assessment has one goal in common: catching a negative or unfavorable trait or characteristic of the business that was not known or disclosed, and verifying assumptions made by the buyer when valuing the business. The confirmatory diligence phase will typically last 45–60 days.

Concentration will typically be discussed. Concentration can exist in your customer base, vendor network, SKU sales or target market, or can be due to seasonality. Other issues are the company's customer and vendor relationships, growth opportunities, backlog, management depth, competitive position, plant capacity, regulatory risks, sales tax risk, unfavorable audits, fines, regulatory issues, environmental issues, and any other matters specific to your business.

Takeaways

- Scrub your financial results going back 2–3 years to ensure there are no surprises embedded in your books and records.

- Critically assess the perceived risks a buyer may have in your business, and identify ways to mitigate those risks. Disclose items that can be perceived as risk to your advisors so they can be introduced properly and at the correct time.

- Be prepared and work from a position of knowledge. Don't leave your deal to chance by trying to sweep issues under the rug.

- Don't let your deal be sabotaged by surprises.

- Be prepared to generate timely and accurate financial information.

Chapter 9
Choosing the Right Buyer

By Jacob Koenig, Managing Director/Partner

WOODBRIDGE
International
Mergers & Acquisitions Since 1993

Jacob Koenig

Once you have interest from a variety of buyers, choosing the best one to transact with becomes the most important decision of the sale process. But how do you know which party is the best buyer? What criteria sets the best buyers apart from the rest of the pack? Do not be fooled—the highest offered price is not the correct answer to these questions. In an auction, you are likely to receive interest from a diverse set of buyers, and not all buyers are created equal. An experienced advisor can help you evaluate the groups that have expressed interest and choose the one that is the most likely to close the deal and do so on the terms you agreed to up front.

So, what are those criteria that your advisor will consider when determining the most capable buyers? Let's explore...

The primary consideration is certainty to close. This means, what is the likelihood the buyer has the cash to do the deal, and can get to the closing table? As a seller, if you are going to agree to an exclusive relationship with a buyer, it is paramount that you know the buyer can get the deal done. Otherwise, you risk losing months of time, energy, and money that could have been spent working with other, more credible groups. Some of the factors that determine a buyer's certainty to close are:

- **Source of cash:** How is the buyer funding the transaction? A buyer that is using cash from their balance sheet or a committed fund has a higher certainty to close than a group that has to raise all of the money from third parties.

- **Track record:** If a buyer has a long track record of doing acquisitions, it is a good indicator that they know what they are doing and have the ability to close.

- **Timeline to close:** In most cases, a buyer willing to commit to an aggressive timeline to close is a stronger choice than a buyer that needs more time. A long closing timeline is often an indicator that the buyer does not yet have the capital lined up and needs time to raise the funds after the LOI is signed.

- **How motivated the buyer is:** A buyer that sees your company as a "must-have" acquisition will prioritize your transaction to make sure they close as quickly as possible.

- **A buyer's strategic rationale:** A buyer with a strategic reason to buy the business will almost always be at the top of the list of ideal acquirers. If that strategic buyer has funded private equity backing, this is even more favorable. This is because a private equity firm is under pressure to buy and build its platform investments. When a private equity platform investment can realize synergies from bolting your business on, this creates the driving motivator for the firm to get the deal done, and done fast.

Beyond certainty to close, you will want to evaluate whether the buyer you are choosing will help you accomplish the goals you laid out when you decided to pursue a sale of your company. Of course, it is important to select a buyer that is offering a fair price for your business, but there is more to consider than that. Two offers with the same headline value might look very different when you dig into the consideration mix. There are several forms of consideration that a buyer might offer:

- **Cash**

- **Rollover Equity:** This is an ongoing ownership stake in the business. It serves to align your interests with the buyer's. With the right partner, the value of this ownership stake can grow substantially and offer you a "second bite of the apple" a few years down the road.

- **Earnout:** An earnout is a future payment (or payments) that are contingent upon the business achieving agreed-upon targets after the sale. Earnouts are typically tied to financial metrics like revenue, gross profit, or adjusted EBITDA.

- **Seller Note:** This is a loan that you make to the buyer. Generally, a seller note will require that your note be subordinated to other institutional debt.

- **Employment/Consulting Agreement:** Although it may not be explicitly included in the valuation a buyer assigns to your business, buyers will often ask a seller to sign an employment or consulting agreement that defines your ongoing role with the company and compensation.

You should look at each type of consideration in the context of your goals. If you want to retire as soon as possible, an all-cash offer with a short transition period is likely your ideal choice. If you are interested in continuing to work and want to share in the buyer's upside, rollover equity (and in some cases, an earnout) can help you achieve that. In these cases, you aren't just selecting a buyer, you're selecting a long-term partner, so it's especially important to be comfortable with the buyer's strategic vision and their ability to achieve it.

There is a vast universe of buyers, especially for small to medium-size companies. It's critical to select an advisor who can help you navigate that universe, and ultimately choose a buyer that has a high degree of certainty to close and will help you achieve the right outcome.

Chapter 10

Management Meeting Training— The One-Call Close

By Andy Gole, Professor/Facilitator

Andy Gole

At management meetings, you meet with bidders who might become your buyer.

The management meetings should result in letters of intent exceeding the amount initially bid, because the management meeting should inject insight and excitement into the process.

Unfortunately, too often we've had a counter-intuitive outcome. We either didn't receive an LOI, or it was lower than the amount bid.

Why was this so?

Studying management meetings, we realized that most sellers had never sold a business and needed substantial coaching on what to say and how to say it at a management meeting to ensure we get the most LOIs with the greatest value.

Thus, Management Meeting Training was born.

Is this possible? You have worked hard all your life to build a close. In a 2–3-hour meeting, it's thumbs up (you get an LOI) or a pass. It's hard to believe, isn't it?

Picture that tomorrow is your first management meeting. You think back on the process that got you here…

The marketing for your business was very effective. Strong bids (LOIs) are coming in. With your closer, you are selecting 3–5 of the strongest bidders for a management meeting.

A management meeting is where you meet with the potential buyers who interest you most. It's the chance for your one-call close.

You are starting to visualize and relish meeting the bidders you have selected and experiencing great management meetings, followed by buyers issuing strong LOIs.

You realize all the preparation you put into the management meeting will pay off.

All too often, management meeting preparation begins 1–2 weeks before the meeting.

But…Is that enough time for the most important sales call of your life?

Not in this process.

You actually have been preparing for management meetings since Day 1.

If you have selected Woodbridge, you enrolled in our two-day/18-hour management meeting training class. At the outset, you questioned the need for the training; selling is selling after all, isn't it?

But you selected this M&A advisor to guide you and this is part of the guidance—the training is essential, so somewhat reluctantly you go.

And WOW! Was it an eye opener!

There were so many issues you weren't prepared to discuss in a management meeting.

Now you have three months to prepare, to possibly make changes that are material and doable.

Here are some of the things you learned in management meeting training: (We call this the company "narrative." It is the past, present, and future of the business.)

- **The importance of your future story:** It's the reason the buyer presented a bid.

- **Your WHY:** What is your purpose, what basic need do you satisfy? This helps buyers understand why customers, prospects, and employees are engaged with your business.

- **Your KPIs:** Key performance indicators—tell the buyer how you manage the business day to day, and make it easy for the buyer(s) to envision owning and managing your business.

- **Your future team:** Who will carry the torch forward? On whom will the buyer rely to manage the business when you step out?

- **Sustainability:** The buyer wants to know that the basic demand for your offering will continue after your step out.

- **Defensibility:** The buyer wants to be confident the competition won't "eat your lunch" once you are gone.

To get a better sense of sustainability and defendability, think of RC Cola. In 1958, it developed the first diet cola. The demand was sustainable to this day. But was it defendable? You don't ask for a diet RC Cola, you ask for a Diet Coke or a Diet Pepsi. The demand was sustainable, but not defendable.

To make it easy for you to present and for the buyer to understand the value of your business, we help you craft and ultimately record an 18-minute TED Talk on your business.

This helps the buyer grasp the whole in a condensed, high-level narrative.

By the end of the two days of training, you will be ready for the first draft of your TED Talk.

Then, when you get to management meetings, the pressure will be off, as you have a polished presentation to begin the meeting. You don't think it's possible?

Miracles happen in our two days of training.

Ask to see an example of a TED Talk, to get a sense of what yours may look like.

Chapter 11

The Importance of Urgency and Tenacity

By Kyle Richard, Managing Partner

By Patrick LaLiberte, Senior Vice President

< Kyle Richard
Patrick LaLiberte >

"Every deal dies a thousand deaths." Inevitably, in every transaction, situations arise that put a crimp in the negotiation. Buyers may suggest a deal go on hold until an issue is resolved. Allowing such a pause is a cardinal sin for a seller. But why?

Successful transactions require a fanatical level of attention on keeping positive momentum and clearing roadblocks. To accomplish consistent momentum requires a sustained and constant sense of urgency, tenacity, and self-motivation. It requires the mindset of not taking "no" as an answer and getting to "yes."

In this chapter, we explain why urgency and tenacity are critical to closing a transaction:

1. **Timing is Everything**

   A buyer may look great on paper, but does that mean a buyer is ready, willing, and able to do a deal? No. Sometimes even the best buyers may not be in the market for acquisitions because of competing interests requiring their attention (i.e., recently completed an acquisition and are focused on integration before adding more). A seller's timing and a buyer's interests do not always line up. Yet, when the timing is right and a deal is struck, there is significant importance to act NOW. The seller with common sense should recognize that he is not the only fish in the sea—and that when a buyer has you on the hook you need to keep them reeling, before another bigger, prettier fish comes along that causes them to cut bait.

2. **Performance, Performance, Performance**

   Most dead deals are a result of material differences from a company's actual results vs. projection; i.e., the seller's business underperformed, and the buyer backed out over the fear the business is a "falling knife." The root cause for the soft financial results might be: (a) the loss of a major customer, (b) an operational issue giving rise to unexpected expenses, (c) a vendor supply issue, (d) or other operational or market forces. It is the seller's job to continue to push the business to achieve the projected results presented in the CIM. It is in the seller's best interest to quickly move to a close, reducing the period of exposure where a negative surprise can arise and negatively impact enterprise value. The longer a deal timeline drags, the more pressure on a seller to maintain growth and consistency of the cash flow and avoid a negative surprise. Note that during due diligence, a seller is answering questions and responding to document requests from the buyer. The seller's attention will be drawn away from his normal focus on running the business and this can cause a decline in performance.

3. **The Buyer's Prerogative**

    The buyer's objective is to minimize risk exposure to the greatest extent possible. One way a buyer will achieve this is by extending the timeline (i.e., the amount of time from LOI to close). The longer a buyer has to "look under the hood," the more likely they are to find an issue. Give a buyer enough time, he may start to see ghosts. Sophisticated buyers will not only review current financial performance, but also the competition, barriers to entry, political risks, regulatory risks, and many more external factors. The more time a buyer has to research and dig, the more time they have to raise potential issues. Then, when a buyer finds an issue, they will use this as leverage to try to negotiate a lower purchase price. This is what is referred to as a re-trade (trading the price down in the later stages of a transaction cycle).

4. **Protecting Yourself from Negatives and Surprises**

    Deadlines are the answer. The establishment of tight timelines determines how the parties will act to get the deal done on a certain date. Deadlines should be created for interim objectives (e.g., completion of Quality of Earnings report, PSA document delivery from buyer to seller). Deadlines allow a seller to gauge buyer behavior and demonstrate that they are focused and committed to closing. A seller must advocate for the parties to march toward those deadlines and clear all obstacles in the way. Remember that this tenacity is generally contrary to what a buyer may desire in a deal cadence. Applying a firm deadline now puts firm expectations in place. It allows a seller to control the process. It limits the exposure of additional risks that can arise out of letting a deal drag.

A seller's preparedness and willingness to make things happen is a massive contributor to a successful transaction. Refer to other chapters of this book for guidance on how to prepare for the sales process. Financial statements should be updated and accurate; legal and operational documents should be available and their delivery expedient. A seller's urgency and tenacity is just as important as the buyer's.

The asset is the seller's asset to sell (not the buyer's asset to buy). A seller can control the tone and tenor of the transaction with how he demands the parties act when the diligence period starts, and control how that process works to protect themselves. The seller having the right attitude and level of energy is key to making the deal work.

Chapter 12

Our People, Our Culture

Positively Transforming the Lives of Business Owners

*By Simon Wibberley, Managing Director, Partner –
Cape Town Operations*

Simon Wibberley

Traditional investment bankers have relationships with buyers. At Woodbridge, the most important relationship we have is with our client, the seller.

Our experience benefits our clients. Since 1993, we have had the privilege of working with every type of entrepreneur from every industry you can imagine. We have used these experiences as opportunities to better ourselves with the net result of benefiting our clients.

We're also early adopters of technology. We believe that taking risks keeps us on the cutting edge and prevents stagnation; and we're not afraid to fail. In fact, we embrace failure. We have learned just as much from our failures as from our successes, and have used those lessons to adapt. Our process of constant review and improvement has enabled us to weather the storms thrown up by changing market conditions over the years. As a result, our tried-and-tested approach to M&A represents innovation at its best.

Meeting Your Team

Your first interaction with our team will be during your kickoff meeting. Even after many years, we still get excited by the moment when a client is greeted by 15 to 20 staff members from Woodbridge, all of whom are excited to learn about you and your business. The scene is generally met with, "Wow, there are a lot of you! I didn't expect this!" Next thing you know, you've connected with a group of people who are going to be instrumental in one of the most important events of your life. And it all starts with a team that is aligned and driven toward achieving a common goal— the sale of your business.

At Woodbridge, the M&A process is divided into specialties. So instead of one person handling your entire sale from A to Z, each person handles one function, and has a broader scope of understanding of their own specialty. A professional business writer writes your book. A professional accountant looks at your books and numbers. A professional closer negotiates your deal and closing. This allows us to customize the work to fit the specific needs of each client. We've learned over time that we get more deals done faster because each person is an expert in their specialty.

Our team is global but very connected. In addition to the U.S., we have a unique team of specialists in Cape Town, South Africa who help us keep our well-oiled machine running 24/7. Like a relay team, they hand projects off to us in the morning, and after hours here, they take over and keep the wheels turning. This helps us keep to our strict 150-day deadline to close. And, a diversity of backgrounds combined with open mindedness and common goals and interests helps us collaboratively drive great ideas every day.

Unique Traits of a Woodbridge Team Member

It all starts with hiring the right people. In the same way you take pride in the business you've built from the ground up, we take great pride in our employees. We recruit meticulously and pick only the people who fit our culture and are invested in developing it.

Woodbridge team members are:

- **Passionate:** Our can-do attitude and positive mindset lead to success for both our clients and the company itself.

- **Entrepreneurial:** We look for people who are innovative, resilient, and willing to take risks.

- **Dedicated and committed:** Our staff understand our sense of focused urgency, and know what it takes to go above and beyond and get the job done.

- **Competitive:** We are a results-driven organization. Winning the mandate, marketing the company, and negotiating the best deal possible motivate us every day.

- **Supportive:** They understand how much you have on the line and are there for you whether your questions are technical or personal.

This is your team! They are ready to support you through the biggest deal of your life.

Chapter 13

The Reasons Our Clients Choose Us

By Neil Dennis, Managing Director New Business

WOODBRIDGE
International
Mergers & Acquisitions Since 1993

By Neil Dennis

"I never want to hear THAT again!"

Years ago, when we were a six-person firm, not the completely different, 75-person firm we are today, we reviewed a small handful of interested buyers with one of our clients. The buyers and their offers weren't bad, but they weren't great either and our client said to us, "Can't you find some more buyers?" While those were words we never wanted to hear again, they continue to inspire us to always seek out new ways to do better for those who place their trust in us. See below the other reasons our clients have chosen us.

It's not who we know or who you know that brings forth the buyer with the best terms, price, and fit, but who shares your passion for the business and your optimism for its future.

We sold a client's business to a buyer whose own enterprise is valued over $20 billion. Normally, this buyer looks for transactions in the ½ billion to billion-dollar range and doesn't take an interest in our clients. In this case, however, they took an interest and had a strategic plan for our client's company. Not only did they beat out six other final bidders, but had the best vision for the future of our client's company. Our client knew no one within the buyer's organization and we knew none of the decision-makers on the buy side, yet our client got the best result.

When buyers you know of show up to bid, it's typically the buyers you do not know that bid up the price for the buyers you do know. So, it is all about how we create a wide-reaching but intelligently curated buyer list to bring the right buyers to our client.

Execution risk matters. We are students of buyers—what they are looking for and how their identity helps predict their behavior and perform for you when it matters most.

While we are open to considering all buyer types for our clients and never like to predict or prejudge who will end up being the best buyer, we'd like to say that not all buyers are created equal at the point at which they execute the LOI and begin the march to the closing date. Ultimately, you pick the buyer, and our job is to educate you on what each buyer—as well as the market—is saying about your business. When we review the bids and the buyers offering those bids, we look at a number of characteristics so we can talk to you about execution risk—the risk, either high, low or moderate—that a buyer will come through in the end.

A pre-engagement value assessment and discussion is one of the most important parts of our mutual exploration. And it is so important that it comes with no cost to you or commitment to us.

So what makes our value assessment different? For starters, we will want to talk about value just as much as you do. So before you hire us, we want to determine our confidence level that your objectives can be met given the circumstances and your desired timeline. The valuation advice we give you is not based situationally on what we think you want to hear or what is going to make you more motivated to sell. Rather than duck the question or shy away from this topic, being able to say "it's too early" or "we are the wrong fit for you or for your company" is why we have been in business 31 years and counting.

Our advice is guided by the thousands of written bids we have received over the years for companies earning $1 million to $35 million of net profit annually in addition to the hundreds of business sale transactions we have completed for our clients.

Many M&A firms and investment banks sold businesses last year. But can they say they received, on average, 20 bids per closed deal?

Successfully completing your transaction is about problem-solving, not about delivering on the promise of a flawless string of events.

While we make great effort to prepare to present your information, defend your financial reports and adjusted EBITDA, and identify items ahead of time that may crop up in a buyer's due diligence, a deal, like your company, is a living entity—it can change unexpectedly from day to day. You might hear from other M&A firms and from buyers who have approached you how smoothly a transaction with them or managed by them will go.

We can't think of one successful transaction where at least one unexpected and also mission-critical issue did not come up. So, when issues do come up, we find it hard to imagine the scenario if we had not prepared as extensively as we did. There will be obstacles blocking the path to the closing date. Legal issues, contractual issues, customer issues, personality issues. Choose us because we have faced many issues and have solved them as a team.

We don't "wing" anything, "guess" or "hope" when it comes to one of the biggest events in your life.

When you hire us, one of the most important game-changing features we will deliver is our 150-day timeline complete with at least 20 intermediary deadlines and a closing date established up front. This timeline used to be 250 days; but over the last few years, we have successfully and continue to eliminate or reduce wasted time in the march toward the closing date. We know how long each task, request, process, and mini-project should take, and we can quickly identify and solve for an emerging problem. The establishment of a timeline with real dates represents a pledge by all parties involved to be accountable to one another and the ultimate goal—the completion of the transaction. Remember, this is your deal and we are on your timeline, not the buyers'.

We let the key people collectively responsible for your transaction carry out the tasks they specialize in and enjoy.

Years ago, Don Krier, one of our cofounders and partners, used to engage with potential new clients, write the offering memorandum and stuff the envelopes with the initial marketing materials. He will readily admit that he did not like writing the memorandums and quite frankly was not very good at it. Many other M&A firms have one or two people assigned to your deal, but we realize it's rare to find one person who can specialize and give their full focus and ownership on each of the various specific tasks. At Woodbridge International, you have a team of specialists.

You do not have to rely only on what we say about our process and our results—we make it easy for you to hear it directly from our clients.

Our job is to deliver on everything we promised. Did bids fall within the range we discussed? Did we adhere to a strict timeline? Did we identify and bring out the best, most fitting, most able buyers? You can get a sense of what it will be like to engage us and for us to bring your transaction to a successful completion in two ways:

Our client testimonial videos—there is a page on our website where we have posted dozens of testimonial videos voluntarily provided by our clients over the years.

Our references—before coming to terms, we would be happy to provide you with a long list of business owners who have successfully sold their business via our process.

Every year we add several new names to that list, and we would be thrilled to have the opportunity to add yours.

Let us know if you have any questions. Best wishes and enjoy the journey.

Notes: